THE SWING GIRL

THE SWING GIRL

poems

KATHERINE SONIAT

LOUISIANA STATE UNIVERSITY PRESS
BATON ROUGE

Published by Louisiana State University Press
Copyright © 2011 by Katherine Soniat
All rights reserved
Manufactured in the United States of America
LSU Press Paperback Original

DESIGNER: Michelle A. Neustrom
TYPEFACE: Whitman

LIBRARY OF CONGRESS CATALOGING-IN-PUBLICATION DATA

Soniat, Katherine.
   The swing girl : poems / Katherine Soniat.
     p. cm.
   ISBN 978-0-8071-3894-6 (pbk. : alk. paper) — ISBN 978-0-8071-3895-3 (pdf.) — ISBN 978-0-8071-3896-0 (epub) — ISBN 978-0-8071-3897-7 (mobi)
   I. Title.
   PS3569.O65396S85 2011
   811'.54—dc22
                                       2011010143

The paper in this book meets the guidelines for permanence and durability of the Committee on Production Guidelines for Book Longevity of the Council on Library Resources. ∞

for Olivia, *Om Namo Bhagavate*

The human is the great and true amphibian whose nature is disposed to live, not only like other creatures in diverse elements, but in divided and distinguished worlds.

—SIR THOMAS BROWNE

Acknowledgments › xi

ONE

Thoughts at Paliani › 3
Hummingbird of Ur › 4
One Wing › 5
Breathing This Long › 6
The Hill Station › 7
Seeking › 8
Nightshade › 9
Self-Portrait with Amnesia › 11
Black Boat › 12
On the Steppes › 13
Impoverishment › 14
The Mark › 15
Geometry › 16
Ferment › 17
Sleeping Alone › 18
Rose Mold › 19

TWO

Flower Viewing › 23
An Aerial Meander › 24
September Sentence › 27
Dahlias › 28
Response to the Rain › 29
The Forest › 30
A Third Way of Seeing › 31
Gravity › 33
Patience › 34
The Wanderers › 35
Day Spool › 36
Solstice › 38
Birthday Crossing › 39
Morning Child › 40
Saint Francis Aubade › 41
Ghost Laundry › 42

CONTENTS

THREE

The Cathedral at Chartres › 45
Cobalt Blue › 47
Painting White Mountain › 48
Cartography › 49
Sickle Moon › 50
Words without a Song › 51
Brocade › 52
The Etudes › 53
Sidereal Travelers › 54
Sleep Interior with Nails › 55
The Rose Salon › 56
Of Aviary Mice and Men › 57
Flight › 58

FOUR

Violets, Lichen, and Bees › 61
Furnishing the Frog Cosmos › 62
The Minotaur's Mother › 63
To the Good Life › 64
The Caldera › 65
The Magicians › 66
Wild Life › 67
The Mind Herder › 68
The Islands › 69
Garden Smiles › 70
Travel › 71
The Swing Girl › 72
Attic Porches › 73
Minoan Apocrypha › 74

ACKNOWLEDGMENTS

Many thanks to the editors of the following magazines in which these poems first appeared:

American Poetry Journal: "Of Aviary Mice and Men" and "The Mind Herder"; *Amicus:* "Impoverishment"; *Arts and Letters:* "Solstices," "To the Good Life," and "The Minotaur's Mother"; *Bitter Oleander:* "Late October" and "The Mark"; *Boston Review:* "The Rose Salon"; *Chelsea:* "Ferment"; *Crazyhorse:* "Saint Francis Aubade" (entitled "Evening with St. Francis"); *Denver Quarterly:* "Eros," "Attic Porches," and "Minoan Apocrypha"; *Georgia Review:* "Morning Child" (entitled "To My Birthday Child"), "Thoughts at Paliani," and "The Caldera"; *Gettysburg Review:* "Flower Viewing"; *Greensboro Review:* "Response to the Rain"; *Hampden-Sydney Review:* "A Third Way of Seeing," "Flight," and "Sidereal Travelers"; *Harvard Review:* "Ghost Laundry"; *Hotel Amerika:* "Violets, Lichen, and Bees"" (entitled "Moss and Violets"), "One Wing," and "The Forest" (entitled "Bees"); *Immortelles: An Anthology of Southern Writers:* "Rose Mold"; *Iowa Review:* "The Cathedral at Chartres," "Hummingbird of Ur," "Travel," and "Furnishing the Frog Cosmos"; *The Journal:* "The Wanderers"; *Kenyon Review:* "Gravity"; *Kestrel:* "Birthday Crossing"; *Mad Hatter's Review:* "Dahlias"; *Margie:* "The Steppes"; *Mississippi Review:* "Nightshade"; *New England Review:* "Painting White Mountain"; *New Letters:* "The Magicians"; *New Orleans Review:* "Black Boat"; *New Hampshire Review:* "Breathing This Long" (entitled "The Fields"); *North American Review:* "The Etudes" (entitled "Blue Oxygen"); *Poetry Daily:* "Painting White Mountain" and "Thoughts at Paliani"; *Prairie Schooner:* "Words without a Song" and "Geometry"; *Red Mountain Review:* "Seeking" and "Brocade"; *Seneca Review:* "Cartography" and "Sleep Interior with Nails"; *Southern Review:* "Rose Mold," "Cobalt Blue," and "Sickle Moon"; *Spoon River Poetry:* "Self-Portrait with Amnesia"; *Threepenny Review:* "Patience"; *TriQuarterly Review:* "An Aerial Meander"; *Virginia Quarterly Review:* "The Hill Station" (entitled "Red"); *Women's Review of Books:* "Sleeping Alone."

Thanks to the Corporation of Yaddo and the MacDowell Colony for residencies which allowed the completion of this manuscript, and to Virginia Polytechnic Institute and State University for their support.

Some of these poems appear in a chapbook, *The Fire Setters;* Web del Sol/Literary Review On-line Chapbook Series.

Dedications for Poems

"The Hill Station" (p. 7), for Pat West
"Birthday Crossing" (p. 39), for Tink
"Morning Child" (p. 40), for my boys: Shelton, Ashton, and Lucas
"Cobalt Blue" (p. 47), for Olivia
"The Islands" (p. 69), for Aimee
"The Swing Girl" (p. 72), for Betsy's Abby

ONE

THOUGHTS AT PALIANI

On the plain below, dozens of cloth windmills spin,
the air clean enough to see through. Like the waterfall you
slipped behind, or left through, years ago.

Light fills the convent garden, the thousand-year myrtle tree
covered with hundreds of hopes for recovery: bright ribbons
knotted to branches while the sick keep faltering.

One wish gives rise to another, and dominoes click in the shade
on a tile table. The nun, who has lived here since she was three,
picks fleas from the dog then pours our thick coffee. The oldest
peer from curtained screen doors. They cook for themselves, eat
alone, and pray for the world.
                                            It's a long stream water makes falling,
each drop coalescing. That spring you died, the moss on the banks
was greener, spray going farther than thought.

HUMMINGBIRD OF UR

Wings fresh from the realm of wild horses. Fast
and faster, one little bird zips through fuchsia,
through the occasional shade of a palm.

Who keeps track of speed in this world
great with spin and fledgling sadness?

Bombing all day, bullets for night. Houses
from the sky must look like hummingbird eggs
to war's polished pilots:
                                  Grid of city blocks, bodies
spread like immaculate dolls on the faraway stretchers.
A newborn's skull closes to such mad fluttering.

The heavy human heart.
Baby and bird turn to ash, and the sun goes down
in its broken-flesh colors.
                                    Exotic, the red gashes halt us. We
linger—second glance at a second world.

Any which garden should be fine for a bird with less than
an ounce of meaning, with a breast
not meant for consumption.
                                  "Filet of hummingbird,"
one poet said over the night grill, her mind watering.
Touch a ghost lightly and dust purples the dirt
where frail things are laid.

ONE WING

Snow on the hills, and the slow sleep begins
that lasts until spring when sunlight pries like a knife—
earth no longer a damp cave but something lit,
with a shifting horizon.

The white one with wings flies by with twigs in its beak.

   dove of long ago that we made prophesy in our rainy
molecular world

   placebo of cool water on our faces   us fumbling around
with thoughts to bring down whatever we could   and anything else
that might follow

   we carried sticks of   and for fire   loaded barrels with gray
powder   hot breath to the match   hot air in the head

   we hung ropes from branches   crushed villages   and spoke
in a broken tongue

   we drew conclusions without a sable brush   or carmine ink
bold sounds for *no* that translated   into *kill*   and apology
this never again will happen

   each phrase had an angle   a catch
that hooked some   and gutted others

   sharpness bit through the leaves   hindquarters   the jaw
snapped in a steel trap

BREATHING THIS LONG

The breath of a cow was scented by the meadows
we hoped one day to return to.
                                          There was an adage
in that province of things collapsing that push too hard
for connection.

The man pointed to the sky overhead, then to the lake
that held the clouds steady. Not far from there, a whole
brigade froze with spring around the corner.

~

They hang the men, the cows
go unmilked, crops in the field burn,
and the young dream of stick coffins.

The sun, at odds with the wind,
sinks.

What gets into those breathing this long
above sea level? The airwaves are jammed
with names for such practiced killings.

THE HILL STATION

Brush fires burn in the valley below, and we talk of hands
in my friend's garden—ceramic palms that rise through the lilies
as though someone were alive in the dirt.

Hands this open and calmed, should the loss of a daughter
be turned loose in this rainless month of wind.

The man from Darjeeling tells of the hill station where a farmer
asked that his hands remain outside the grave
                                            to show he left
with nothing.

Flute notes lift from the rapids, and on the trellis a buzzard skeleton
winks its Christmas-light heart. Red again, then dark.
Jewel in the bone tree.

My friend wonders what this man from far away will make of her art
and handmade quarters—river stones mortared in as flooring,
wooden rail for the steps, a twisted polish of rushing water.

And behind the house is the barn she moved uphill, board by board,
to hold her paintings. One canvas hangs in the loft—

pointillist's net-of-a-cat poised among the cardinals.

SEEKING

Prayer smoke that curls
Ash on the altar
Sand garden to rake

Hands that press skyward   the rock face to climb.

What man makes in the sun
What he's made of the Earth.

The animals we are is a law stuck in nature.
Visages savaged by beadcarving, bloodcut,
And maskrut—maps of how we got this far.

In a lit circle, drums lead us to trance
To stare at the navel.
That's not what a monkey watches in the green leaves.

The mind goes up like a kite. In the air we drift,
Enchanted by such a grand station. Hands extended,
We seek piously, fervently
                           like a tank's roving gun
That stops on the man by the town fountain. One good
Kill among many. Another body to trash while the living
Take to the streets, each faced with learning, back to the wall,
Mouths floodlit and railing.

NIGHTSHADE

Rain hardly stopped the month of August, kettle boiling
on the stove for tea. She decided to give in, as a painter might,
and let shadows offer direction. She'd follow with a sponge,

dab gold at the edges.

At least the dusty Chevy in the drive was washed and ready for travel.
Sometimes she thought of it as her ticket past the rural drive-in

where stars kissed beyond the hood, and she drove home

to prowl the warm black fields with the cat.

Today she found a title for evening made from her dreams,
Baby Elephant in the Choir Stall. After close-ups of deep red
puckers under the Milky Way, and a summer of Bach weaving
from her hallway into the mist,

why not an image this ungainly, waving its wrinkled nose at the future?

The trick was to solve the puzzle of a liturgical young elephant—
this animal, a first trumpeter of song.
                              Then came the training, the chaining,
and poking at a life to make it fall in step and be quiet.

And here she had an elephant who closed its eyes and napped in her dream.

She stopped in the middle of tea on a wet afternoon. How had Bach
and a clean Chevy suggested such travel?
                              Imagine how this creature
would sound years from now, fully awake in a cathedral.

Echoes of all the long-held *misereres*.

There was such persistence in this image, it was similar to those
of the Chinese artist she'd known who painted canvas after canvas
of empty train stations in pre-war Berlin—

                                          glass dome, the rails beneath
crisscrossing like comets, flare of the city through an archway.

Night-sheen drew him, though he knew the paints, bought in Beijing, over time would disappear. Sometimes he filched soft tar from road gangs in his province.

How would it be to sit on a bench in one of his depots? She could wear her favorite black scarf and know with each breath she was fading a bit, going away.

SELF-PORTRAIT WITH AMNESIA

The face is blank on the canvas, an oval
she painted herself out of—the orange gladioli
intersecting her jaw-line.

It doesn't take much to see she's forgotten
about summer, the evening light and wandering

the mountains.
Without a mouth, she's not partial to sighs,
and there's not a sound from the conch shell

beside the vase of tall flowers.
What told her that day to trade the blue notes

for no eyes at all, then to leave out the lips
with their swings at happiness?
The hair's adrift with the same spidery strokes

that barely suggest her hemline and gold slippers. Shoes,
a reminder of the ground she covered.

Call her *tabula tacit*, say she's the primary silence.

Those who stare long enough find darkness expansive.

She must have been conceived by the mind anciently

dilating. Figure scratched on the cave wall, missing
its orifice and sockets.

BLACK BOAT

I heard you call my name years after
we parted. Summer in the mountains,

I looked up from weeding and saw only
a crow. That said, your dying began,

stopped, and commenced again. The year spent,
black boat with its red sail set in motion.

It was quiet the day I heard you,
nobody there but that solitary bird.

Some years start in black and white,
and by October scarlet enters in.

Leaf and sky were the shades I learned
with you. Now I keep a place in the pines

for the sun to slip through.
Why did we settle, uneasy, rock-heavy,

but not of rock?
At dawn, deer snort outside the bedroom window,

and half asleep I say, Oh hush, as if to a child.
Brain filled with morning air, my metabolizing

old organ awake to scold again, demanding
even of these deer.

ON THE STEPPES

He moved to another level, looking for a place to stop
the thoughts.
For days I watched him on his journey
then emptied a cellophane of stars,

silver and gold

dropping

down through a dying man's tea.

Hermits in a pale universe,
each fleck scattering to a dimension
where it is good to be less.

I saw his eyes begin to wander the room like a town. We joined forces,
no hint of light on the streets, nothing to amuse or sadden. The sole movie
was captioned in another language, Lear in embattled black and white.
In Russian, he raved on the steppes,

motioned the wind not to turn its back.

IMPOVERISHMENT

Summer in the empty pasture,
wagon ruts overgrown long ago.
Fence posts topple across the valley—
nothing much left to enclose.

The book of fluke, wing, and flesh is finished.
Whale, cockatiel, and the world's long line
of hungry children gone,

labeled "species impoverishment."

Ghettoed, shot, zooed, they disappeared like a swarm
of cosmic frictions nobody wanted.

Bonfires commemorate, the surveyors designate,
naturalists record.

                No one stopped to gaze for the beast:
what it must have been to dwell on the trees   breathing seeing
then closing the eyes   only to return to the same
spot in the leaves.

THE MARK

Orioles fuss in the feeder,
blossoms of bloodroot opening beneath.

In the woods, chain saws whip the air to pine dust,
the forest floor soon a marker for the missing shades
of spring.

Last night a dog struggled in the high seas of my dream.
His panicked, deep-water bark.

Head up, he was swimming hard, paddling toward me,

and I held as much damp green air as I could.

GEOMETRY

Stones sit on the moonlit platter.
I water them to make the night glitter,
fuchsia blowing, the neighbor's cat
on the porch dabbing at her reflection.

The mind takes to color like sugar,
this, my paltry day-of-the-dead set out
for drowned sailors—

limestone, agate, and amber under water. Picked
from the sand for their whimsy, each holds an image—

smudged sail on a Chinese junk, white curled to gray
on another.

Half and half of the universe.

So when the clink, clink of cocktails begins at three a.m., I expect
plum wine and laughter, not five raccoons groping at water. The biggest,
looking, chunks down on the deck—one, two, three of its wish-fish
gone awry on a clear summer night. Deep realm of indelible pattern.

FERMENT

I carry them from the cellar where they sat all summer
in a soup carton by the furnace. Bright jars of brandied peaches

like ones from years ago in the pantry window,
my mother's red wallet by the bourbon, so she could find it
in the morning when the house grew quiet.

But those aren't these that come from days when,
living for our bodies, we were made of syrup.
Quarts of liquored fruit I carry upstairs, the soft-boated
sex of each pitted peach, and I want our eyes to meet again
and hold steady.

After all, it is the end of October and yesterday a black cat
named Cinderella took one look, then followed me purring
into the red leaves.

SLEEPING ALONE

After lunch in the woods I was sleepy—
long fingers in stream water, and beneath
spread the mica's blurred silver.

Though it was noon, an owl breezed by with a snake,
and I lay in the shallows.

The creek was a place for rest that summer,
its stones a mortar, each housing the flash of a face
or figure beneath water.

I fit as a rock after years in the garden, wondering
how empty a bed must be for me to get in. The sky's
strewn with heavenly bodies, a pointillist's dilemma.

Snakes,
stars,
salt glow of another shore—
each bedrock thing dispersed with slowly
as the water moves by.

ROSE MOLD

The month of July I held the door open,
and in walked the spider for my forehead.

Hornets came to snip at my wrist, and while
I picked roses, thorns stuck the flesh till it blushed

with poison. Rose virus in my veins. I'd been pricked
by life in the yellowing fields, as one by one my animals

vanished in the woods. I was swollen and empty, and thought
of the man who tended bushels of roses, red and gold tantrums

on the vine. At the end, he had vases of them carried
from his room. Those roses he had looked at and thought of

for so long hurt him—their buds, the gardened air. In the spotted
petals by his bedside was beauty on its way to being mystery.

TWO

FLOWER VIEWING

Like the thirteenth-century nun, Abutsu,
I began to see blossoms with my eyes
closed.

Blue petals swayed above the dirt,
August tomatoes came to mind
on the heels of the little red cat.

They too were part of the dwelling I carry
on top my neck all summer. I balance it
and them on a stem without support.

Unlike the Japanese scholar locked in a room
to read for days and nights, for weeks with a rope
tied around his throat to jerk hard and sudden

should he doze away from the thoughts of others.
Meanwhile, flower-viewing parties gathered
on a night with no moon.

AN AERIAL MEANDER

> Not to break frail bones, many of the nineteenth-century elderly were wrapped in down quilts, and told to stay in bed for the winter.

Sky filled with geese and snow. Whiteness clouds down
on the fire-builders rummaging through brush,
trying to hide something.

Enough softness here for a small village to bury its old in.
Body-wrap of quilts and sheets,
years of flesh packed up like the good bone china.

The frail bed down under the Wolf Moon,
light silvering the rooftops. Such a celestial lid
to cover the agéd with.

Told to go to their rooms and stay,
the old become Olympian dreamers of a cold season.
Wise enough to know the spare room and slop pot

are not invitations to stay another month,
another minute, one woman sinks into her feathers
at dusk, and pulls up the covers.

Pillows surround her like re-embodied fowl.
She thinks of fleeing farther than the farthest farm,
her years of habitation trailing behind

as the shaking off of life begins.
Her heraldic bones break through the cloud cover,
flick everything brassy in the heavens aside.

Rib, hip, and pelvis roll through the sky.
Then the tornadic rush
at what's left:

her boneless flesh sucked in,
made small as a blood-red dot.
Clothed as a scarlet midget,

she is war's soul caped in the shadows.
Sun pours through artillery holes,
a river thaws with the dead. It swims with them.

Lightness swirls in her head. Beneath her cloak,
tiny pricks to her shoulder, pinions thrust in each pore
until slowly she rises

to fly.
No longer the lone heart in a stone bunker,
she is aerial meander of a certain kind.

Below, they point and hungrily yell *goose*
as she flaps by.
Wings over the stained land,

over corpses no different from boulders on the moon.
One hangs from a tree like carcass on rafters.
From the barns of cutlery comes the shout,

hold the throat back, cut quick like a pig's.
The sky reddens. Mouths fill with lame calls
to anyone—the flame-throwers, the fire-builders

intent only on running
at one another.
Then the heaviness, the absolute pull

of inertia comes upon her. Levity
collapses, frozen
in sunlight.

She is pounds of gooseflesh,
yellow skin on waning muscles.
Time is up,

down,
all over her,
sinking her to the ground again.

Feathers fall to where the hurling, thrusting
arms have tired, have worn themselves to pieces—
appendages that could have been wings.

SEPTEMBER SENTENCE

Uncut corn in the field,
Raucous vultures tossed on the sky,

Human caravans fleeing.

Every day is as relentless as a plow pushing
Them to the edge of a mountain,

To the brink of this processed, cleansed,

Mop-the-blood-off-the-deck world

Where one summer men arrived
With mouths full of nails,

And shovels to dig a hole for part of the race
To rot in. Then they pound the ground shut.

DAHLIAS

Stones covered our notes in the garden,
a thought for each week
you were ill.

One star above the blue lake
and I began to wonder how you'd ever return,
the horizon discrete even then.

The story of the mountain always points somewhere
else, elusive as the tawny lion disappearing behind
the next high crag.

RESPONSE TO THE RAIN

My student writes in her journal that when the story's point of view
shifts from first-person to the dog's, that represents the "third eye"
perspective.
                    What wisdom wanders this stuffy office—a pup
who won't give in to peripheral vision. Nor does he ponder
his last bad master or latch onto the thought of a bone.
Nose down, he slips through the wet morning.

THE FOREST

I sold my car to the woman who at first hesitated over a dent
in the fender, asking when was my "most recent big collision."

Then counting twelve dried bees strewn across the backseat,
she added it looked as though the car had gone through

a forest of bees, only to correct herself,
"or is it that your car is a forest of bees?"

So, is my car part of the great arboreal realm,
and exactly what did she deduct for each of those

weightless gold flaws? One day I'll visit her country's
moss gardens to find my old gray Toyota mulched

in with the shade.

A THIRD WAY OF SEEING

Years from now imagine walking barefoot through the trees, tall and windy.
It's best to be quiet enough to hear the leaves touch,
                                                      then study one ant's
indirection, the flat-footed pedestrians never suspecting your last
shaky teacher.

~

Some say what we need is more backbone, the marrow of refusal. The curled brain
asks for nothing but safety—
                                a thousand times over we do the same thing,
deluded on Sacred Mountain.

~

The record book is fragrant with juniper. Curtains tied back on the family kitchen,
the kettle boils from last night when words careened and belittled,
                                                              then fell quiet
to make room for the small red being born with a heartbeat.

~

Least wise of the unwise, we who place ourselves above the herd, but not
beneath the stars. The bent beast stares at the drinking pool—blank eyed,
the past undigested.
                          Empty-headed, it rushes forth like wind sucking snow
from the cliffs. Who sees the mutant frog that wears the pond's weather?

~

The garbage adds up. Heaped under the snow, it swells along routes to peaks
hewn by the ages. Now there's a cold that makes the bones shine and the vulture's
eye brightens.
                    Ivory and ebony. Chance sighting of two birds that doubles to four.
Each climber lives by the last calculation. Frozen corpse is a load to cart
off the mountain.

~

Find the zenith that holds, then look down where there's no end to trouble; where most often I have only a minute, maybe an hour, today let go of, godforsaken, until we meet in the depot.
                                        Glass dome on a crowded station. You peer up and say it makes you remember. Remote union with some spot past me in the sky.

GRAVITY

That day I saw the clock without us,

its pale enamel face wiped clean.

The maple was a different shade from last year.

I stood there thinking how a tornado does not rush through
but takes one rough bounce down,
then another.

The closet mirror lay in the woods,
stones around its sunlit surface.

One red leaf at the center of reflection.

I wanted to root that leaf, to watch the light move in and out—
fall wine on my tongue to swallow, the moss below damp
like a pet's grass-scented belly.

I began to feel as clear as water
but with that heaviness
too.

Wind on the mirror.

PATIENCE

On the asylum path, the groups of eight move daily,
up to the sign—End Patient Walking Area. Then medicinally,
methodically, they return, the hospital filled each morning
with screams from a seventh-floor window.

The walkers hear that cry, but look at me and my dog,
hoping sooner or later I'll let him live under their beds.

For small change and cigarettes, they're sure I'll give him away.
At night they mull him over and come back with fantasies,
with dimes and tobacco until one of their oldest disappears.

Helicopters swoop the woods, searchlights the creek. By sunup,
a man wanders from the trees, says he's been sitting on a rock,
feeling the night pass with the wind. He blows a smoke ring,
flips me a coin for what runs loose in my dog, a thing that
knows no composure in the green moonlight.

THE WANDERERS

After the earthquake a woman insists everything
has settled down but the ground and that she knows

what to save and how to do it.
                              From station to station,

all afternoon on the radio, she wanders through the news.
Not a tree or flower in her yard has lost its balance, while

down at Divinity's the French perfumes were uninsured,
as was the jade vase that landed in a heap.

                                        By evening on TV,
her withered voice attaches itself to the face and little laughs

of this woman who tries hard to carry on with certainty.
I turn her off and roll over to sleep in my own cracked

kingdom:
         The ground a hard glaze, wind full of sleet, I skid

through a mountain pass, while behind me trek a diminutive
tribe of the weirdly familiar, careful to step

only where I do.
                Like something forgotten, my feet are saviors

we look to to lead us from this high-goat world. Ice fields shine
on every side.

A bear skull appears, mouth open wide with yellow teeth.
Then its ribs show, pressed to the cliff like a creature flattened

in a freeway tunnel.   *Oh, city bear,* I call, *poor lost fossil.*

DAY SPOOL

        windchime

morning fling   bells ring
wood deck   wood peck   hood red   ruby head

      meadowglaze   dew maze
            lake rind

spunshine

      ~

        windtime

noon-high sunsquash
            spool slow
                amberwash

      dayslip plum blip
   peargold   goddess old

      ~

        windchime

twilit
          lost flight
                cloud showers
                shadows tower

vision trimmed
        dream scrim

~

windchime

keeps time

    heart starts   :   breaths part
       moon sweeps tree deep

birds gone
quiet.

SOLSTICE

Hemlocks in the rain-green valley,
clubs of insects meteor the lake,

and blue eaves for every bush of sunlight.
How exacting summer was.

Beyond that,
a woman walked out on another cold year.

Like a sheet of ice held to the light,
she disappeared from the window,

then from that town.
Into the hours came the children

walking home through shadows
until one saw, and began the orphan call.

Darkness rises, sometimes the sun falls.
A man kills wildflowers by the tracks for a living.

That lucky old sun turns on us certain days,
and rolls far north of heaven.

Night's a bone press. But think how the skull
used to cock in the daylight, the eyes dream openly.

Some sleep alone, beyond the sing-song ways
of little ones.

First up the lake tower on solstice eve,
a woman listens for the children. Far past

our tropic of this or that, polar baths
overflow with sunshine, then pitch.

BIRTHDAY CROSSING

Tonight I walk through snow to the pond,
into the years where I go on,

and you stopped.

Think of all the failed mother-daughter sets,
their machinations ended as they detached

and flew through space, nothing but cold

in their opening, closing arms. Something
calls for an end of pairs. Still, lovers come

looking for the familial.

Like children, they long for replica—
fish shadow beneath the ice, the pool of untouchables.

In dream you surfaced as the sea-spouting whale,

the ocean poured skyward, and I felt the maternal,
tidal heartbeat.

Years ago, I watched you, a woman my age now,

die in the bed where you were born. I knew that
moment and what was happening was unstoppable.

Standing by the falls in the woods,

I sometimes think that if I stay long enough,
they'll come to a halt. Like water, the memorized body

goes on. Our fifty-four turns around the sun.

MORNING CHILD

After our shadows joined hands
bringing out the dark, I was time

smoothing my palms across your
breathing face. I traced tales of cloud

shapes until you believed in sleep.
You slept, waking at dawn for me

to give the day a name. I was Monday
full of roles and hours full of light.

You kept a corral for the sun, rode it every
moment it could stay. It was always time

to crack open the world—the second spring
of a reindeer, rubbing trees and gladness

forming in your head.

SAINT FRANCIS AUBADE

Before his fast was broken, he courted strangeness,
not the oncoming world's hair and wet gizzards.

Just to sit a bit longer on the cliff with the star
he pinpointed the hours by with one, then the next,
branch of pine.

He marked the dirt when near and far
made a brief union.

Star and loblolly hitched in the pink shell of space.

Then he thought of the bilious living—goatskins of wine,
the tight bodices—with so much emptiness spread out

above him.

        Such heights made him waft, like
a butterfly. Looking down,

far down at the valley
                he felt his lungs
inches high, ounces heavy.
In-and-out, the two quivered.

For moments, he was a masterwork with the tapping heart.

GHOST LAUNDRY

By fall they brush up against us, almost flapping
with scent, these absences that are constant and faithless
in the same breath.

Like heathens, we can't believe our abandoners
and want more than the solar drag of wind on the clothesline.

After a heavy rain, apples wash by in the ditch, turtles
head for the road, a meeting place for the high
and low.

I watch clouds shadow fields of sunflowers,
that golden crop that follows beginning
to its end.

Why our need to stop things
in mid-air, as if the waterfall could refuse more?

One night you said you could see her smile again.
The smile she wore, a worn smile
like the beaten path that stays well after the garden.

THREE

THE CATHEDRAL AT CHARTRES

Here's the great doorway,
there, a bride so far away she's a trail of light.

Small woman, tiny groom set out
to commune at the end of a stone universe.

Today, all of her good saints
are an ordinary mix

of decayed plant and animal,
this nuptial an arranged potion

of tulle, rose, and candle haze.
Soon she'll turn to drag her long train

out to the street.
From the doorway I peer through the dankness,

the end of a hot summer morning
on my back.

Row after row of polished pews,
then there they are again, my altared bride

and groom. The organ pours harmony
over this pageantry of humans. Smiling,

the gargoyle has overseen countless plans,
these primary conciliations of men

and women. He's seen so many
he could doze off above his walled garden

of platitudes. Or he could compose a heart
with rhythms to inspire any idea of grandiosity.

Snort of a bannered crusade, sea-weary sighs of Magellan—
those brief exhalations when two or more gather to believe

there'll be no future such as theirs.

COBALT BLUE

When what was mine was six weeks old,
the long legged chimney-bird stood in the lemon grass.
No swaddled baby swung from this stork's beak.

No virgin tale to tell. Only my story in autumn of you
landing for the first night alone in your crib.

An owl flew by the frosted cabin window, foxfire in the brush.
Piercing cries at water's edge, then the subtler notes with first light
in the trees.

You slept under blankets, a goldfish in a bowl by the curtain.
Two breaths, ripples moving in and out on the marsh. The wind.

Our home in cobalt blue I called it, place-name for this sphere
in the void—porch by the side of the road, wind chime
with whole and quarter notes colliding.

PAINTING WHITE MOUNTAIN

Wang Wei's snow is prepared,
a saucer of crushed oyster shell.

He looks out the window, pulls a screen
across summer.

All morning he renders the peaks
calcified by the *skull-bone* stroke.

Wrinkle-in-the-devil's-face
is saved for the deep ravine.

Each cleft adds dignity to rock,
small resting places on the long way up.

Crystals blow in from the west. Remote,
these plains where one could stretch out forever.

He goes to his cot in afternoon. By four o'clock,
the footpath appears he has pondered for days.

Tracking the travelers, he paints their retreat,
dim as a cave with a bell at its heart.

Few leaves remain on the maple. His wrist,
a guide to the snow—whiteness falls on boiled

and beaten silk. He hears the monks' slow chant.
Frost on a ledge honors that voice,

his hut abandoned by autumn.

CARTOGRAPHY

The trip surfaced slowly that brought us around the lake
then up to a cabin on the hillside. My son and I took the old road
away from town and the deserted bus barn, past the organized sleep
of people living together.

We were at a loss that March, looking for the right place
to go. As if from space, we watched emerging land and the thin
blue lines appear. Maps spread on the kitchen floor. At our feet,
ads for peaks, rivers, and old hotels. So exact, I thought something
had to happen next on a mountain by a lake.

We'd almost reached a decision, when I saw my son look over
his shoulder at the bedroom door. I wanted to say, *Look, if we
can please get to one outcome...* as though that green
fishing fly were not poised on the trash, and beside it the suit
his father had dreamed of over and over at the end,

dreamed of stroking as it hid behind a confessional curtain,
only to reappear in radiant form, high above the altar. Doubting Thomas,
dying, he struggled with the invisible one moment, the untouchable the next.
And I sat watching a road lead off the map toward that suit folded
by the door, ready to be given away.

Afternoons, the bus barn down the street stirs with pigeon wings,
birds in gray vestment. Neighbors bang screen doors with apologies,
threats. Words that foreclose or predict. On days like that, we studied
maps on the floor, mountains beyond the water.

SICKLE MOON

The caption reads *Without Her Violin Bow*
and suggests what once-in-a-blue-moon did
to the woman at the table—

                              that never-never moon,
the pale birthmark of what seldom should happen.

The room empties of roses, her fiddle stick is gone.
So how can she make music (or love for that matter)
in such legendary silence?

                              Her tongue is tied
for as long as war will take to poke its knife
through every young girl's window.

At galactic heights, the milky splash of stars evolve.

She has so much space (and so little time) to consider a light
in the barracks window, brass-buttoned soldiers lined up
and ready to fall.

                              Battalions have twinkled through that hallway.
She learns to sleep on one leg, balance gone between the moon
and water.

WORDS WITHOUT A SONG

A week after the killings, I read an overview
of the elegy. The long thin call of birds

plays in the background; that CD
where a man's voice interrupts to name

each feathery blue-and-gold composer.
All day the airwaves shatter with freshly

arranged terms for war, for retribution and
slaughter.

The sky holds above, earth below—
foiled, silent horizon.

And us trampling the middle air
where amaranth first brightens the rubble.

BROCADE

A spider web on the fence sections off the farm
with angled gray glitter. Evening sun for a while
until the elemental curl of a tornado
sways from the west—sunflowers
and prairie dog whiskers, manure
caked on yesterday's trowel,
chicken droppings and corn
silk are part of this
high-flying
compost.
              Dirty twin to the waterspout
funneling light down through the centrifugal
fish flying. Vaporizer from an asthmatic's
pale childhood changes
dry air to liquid.

Earth, sea,
and wind
stood on end
stand at odds with the horizon.

On a small lit scale, the whole's recollected.

THE ETUDES

She heard the pines—
their cold shade, like some part
of the spectrum,
fractured.

How quietly he left the circled hours
with their snow-globe fury.

By late March, longing uncurled,
root-haired in the dark, her brush
with spring imminent.

Chords of ice-melt on the river,
leaf rot risen to its highest power.
Sometimes Chopin's Etudes addressed it best,

his piano focusing any uncertainty. Octaves and
arpeggios, undulations she took as an invitation
to hush.

All she had to do was be there—
death, a low blue echo with her world on top,
the breeze flying March glitter.

For weeks after a spade turned the dirt back
and filled it in again, his hillside grave lay raw
above the creek.

Nothing to do but throw a line out to the wind—
kite string, bow line—anything that flies forward.

SIDEREAL TRAVELERS

mountain time

The winds were high when I thought I saw you bathing in the creek. Your flesh changed colors with moonlight.

Lanterns blew on the ridge all night, beacons for the sidereal travelers.
I scooped watery stars to touch the silent dimension. In crevices and on the stone

path, more than dream moved on an empty stomach.

pacific time

An unstrung harp in the window, waves wash in far below. Days and
nights stretch before this continent, before one room filled with ocean wind

and a broken harp—the air made shapely in an unintended way.

So many sighs start off across the water; the horizon an unborn blue,
and always out of reach.

SLEEP INTERIOR WITH NAILS

Up the basement stairs he comes with wash in one hand
and a hammer in the other.

Outside, three gray foxes slip beneath the clothesline
then head for the woods.
                          The weather calls for more
damp blue, and the sheets are still too full of the ocean.

Eleven nails glisten from the crown of his head,
pounded from the inside out. Touching each point,
he counts them, smiles and keeps rising
through the stairwell.
                    Twenty acres, a few cows and
horses run through his mind—part of an older scheme—
the laundry clouding beneath them, rain folded in
with sodden cottons.

Through a long line of evening showers he climbs,
getting nowhere, unlike doughnuts that roll down the stairs
from a bag of hot air.
                    The same dozen he gobbled as a kid
after holy communion. As if to confirm, a nun billows by,
says she's come to recall guilt for a child. But she's so proud
of her boy, all grown now with a head full of nails, and not hair.
One of God's wives poking fun at the willful.

And all he wants to know is how far it is past the clothesline
to the foxes; how many more lifetimes before he reaches
the forest interior.
                That settled, the nails begin to glow, dreamlike,
dampbright. Foxes make room in the trees, rain reddening
the plowed September field.

THE ROSE SALON

Ninety-six roses she takes in for May at a business
where she cut people's hair. Eight dozen stems

sent by eight different men, our lady of petals, a hot
new commodity after moving out on her boyfriend,

who's still an avid contender. To be pursued with such
a flourish of flowers. Each man she led to the basin,

head back, throat arched while she massaged the skull's
phrenology. Then, off went the locks of her biblical

Samson. A potent condition, this month of May—
roses multiplying, the silver shears flying. Air thinned

to quotidian essence, and all she can do now is smile
at the vases. But then, as if prodded by love too smoothly

conceived, she dreams of a land not made for lovers,
and she, no Lysistrata, has not the foggiest notion

how to stop the oncoming slaughter.

OF AVIARY MICE AND MEN

Hickory dickory dock,
parakeets nap at the top,

the mice below simply delight
with seed left out overnight.

Wild bees, honey and wax,
tea on the ramparts by buttery lamps.

Ransacked, an emperor's chamber,
stone walls for the strong to dismember.

Terra cotta soldiers stacked in the tomb,
porous guards for the afterlife's battles.

Silk banners and saintly elixirs
make light of our ravenous species.

How can we comprehend history? See here,
billions of molecules scroll down as a spring mountain.
Know there are no roads back, no ladders. Dropped
seed, the thing left in context.

FLIGHT

Old mountains.
Vast men
See beauty at its beginning,

The earth tilting upwards
Then down to a valley at noon.
Their eyes take excursions

Out over the plains and ridges.
They linger on a dying pine.
Musical molecules drift from a hawk,

Air worthy of being breathed in—
Counterweight to the high monastery,
Its candled window.

FOUR

VIOLETS, LICHEN, AND BEES

Would it help to breathe the loam deeply . . .
Earth is one brief ceremony then another.

Cycles of more cold-blooded sparring at sea-level . . .
Ocean's the last of our frothy, whipped summer gardens.

And what if she had slept in the field of rainy coreopsis . . .
Consider being alone in a feathered place.

Like when she started talking again, the phone cord damp
in her hand, the bed softly doubled beneath her . . .
*See it as seasonal regression, the grief muscle in the brow moving,
growing stronger.*

Maybe that's why she saw him in dream, saying he looked more
rested than alive—those deep white circles beneath his eyes . . .
*It's different being in the clockwork stillness of a stucco house
where things get better or worse, but never are done.*

What to do with the supine intimacy of her bed and the phone
no one answers . . . *Chalk it up to another world—the waves
washing out, bee on a reed, foghorn at noon.*

FURNISHING THE FROG COSMOS

Earth-jam of a mulched garden—foxglove and iris
beneath the statue that trickles water from her jug
into the pond.

Frogs by the lily pad couple, aloof, eggs adrift
in the green algae.
                    Why shouldn't offspring of a given moment
be kin, whatever it takes to link lives across the species?

Think of these squiggly scribbles on water, the young translucent
ones preparing for the planet, for clumsy leaps through circles
of slime.
              And not far from here in the woods, the discarded clothes
of childhood lay buried—softened shoes, patched woolens and denim.
An owl dives for the red-headed woman as she weeds a small plot.
Her fickle mane is something that bird wants, sweaters clumped
underground with the wingéd mittens.

In a flash, that woman rises, out of synch with the concrete maiden
who pours water endlessly for the frogs.
                              One by one, the stories
diminish, an outgrown body of clothing at home in the dirt.

THE MINOTAUR'S MOTHER

A white bull wades in the pond, and Pasiphaë
wants him more than human reflection.

He snorts.
        Part of her gives way, fingerlings
swirl through the reeds, as down she goes
to a vast universe.

All the starry shoot-to-shoots open, each arranged
constellation
unhinged:
        Bear and the sisterly Pleiades
set out to prove nothing.

(And wouldn't this be stunning to see from the sky—
shoreline emerging packed with the tuberous lilies,
bull and woman on our moonstruck planet?)

So who tattled (and passed the word) on Pasiphaë,
wife caught in horror
as she lifted her haunches?

TO THE GOOD LIFE

Of feta, green oil, and black olives.
The waves ride high for Ondine

Who thrives on each spumey motion.
Of The Residential Moby-Dick Bar and

Breakfast, another anomaly rising from the Aegean.
Of cliff cave, goat gorge, and the fisherman's

Pet goose that won't stop hissing
While fresh squid is rolled in cracked pepper.

Of a white bull not named Minotaur,
Free from our violent and mythic occasions.

THE CALDERA

Memento mori sit in a glass cabinet
on the woman's grave: can of Ajax,
bottled Coke, and "Windex" labeled
on a baby-food jar—accompaniments
of a life, as rock upon rock tumble
down the caldera.

No ossuary chambers are sealed above the sea.
No cunning spouts for genies to lift from.
Gone, the clear stream with wood-nymphs
clad in shadows.

Still, the Ephemera come and go. Tonight
it's a funeral regatta where the black sails
turn white with deception,
                            and the crowd goes wild
at the mention of Hieronymus Bosch. Then a big laugh
when they discover that the man who wants me back

is dead. And here I am wondering how long I should

tell him to wait or to grow his hair

if that's all he's got going.

THE MAGICIANS

> . . . Crete, isle of many trees and deep shade
> —HERODOTUS

Half fox, part goat, this statue stands at the inlet
where boats once set sail for the sun or the dead
to float home in,

another day   old and ending in the cedars.

It's spring overhead and twilight in the forest.
Not a good time to see clearly . . .
a time to think more   like water,

                    the ghost-elders
loose in the wind
their shadows left on a branch, waiting.

Sparrows drop twigs into the lustral bath's oil of rose attar—
rainbows for the cleansed, ceremonial body.

In the branches birds flutter and jerk. Clumsy dance
of mating.

Quiet settles on the estate of an evening magician.
Haunches of goat and the sly pointed gaze of a fox.

WILD LIFE

The one who leaves does not stay away. It's his calm face
in dream with the tantrum-red innards of another: two male

lovers in flesh of her own making. And she can't stop sleeping
with them, caught between longings.

Strange, that a man this diminished would be good cover
for wild life to hide in until morning when the path next door is

swept clean. Swish, swish beneath the lamb hung from a rope
on the butcher's balcony. He argued past midnight, then slammed

out the door. Today the bay sparkles, and the skinned body becomes
a bit less in the wind. Torn thing, twenty feet up on a cord

reminiscent of muscle.

THE MIND HERDER

She waits for as long as sunset takes to part
with its pale pet clouds.
                        The familial hours
done, her moss-clad twin comes for the night.

It's dizzying to keep the two straight, the pursuer
and the one bound to flee.
                                Silence starts where the body
ends, and tonight begins with her tongue dying
to touch as she catches the goat-boy's eyes—
swarms of lapis above his candle
at the cave bottom.

Down on his haunches, he's coaxing. The flute opens

(like her thoughts) to his fingers.

The herding notes
wander.

His eyes are blue. The walls are wet limestone.
A stalagmite shape some call a woman rises
with its drip-by-drop little ones building up
in the mud.

He holds light to each secretion. Village fool,
goatherd, or clown? She follows his leaps from ledge
to ledge, his eyes, and hindquarters.

THE ISLANDS

At the peak-shrine I drink water from a cow horn,
the oleander gorge muddied by the first rain in weeks,
fishing boat in the distance.

Here, a sunny mountaintop; there, the cave where hundreds
of feet down in the dark my eyes grew big and found nothing.
Now a bucket of roses sits in the chapel ruins.

Clouds shadow the island to the north. Last night I swam
for it, drawn to a lantern on the hillside. *Favma,* I thought, my hand
out of the water and pointing out "miracles."

White caps ruffle the afternoon sea, and I'm slick with dream
slowly dissolving. *Hazio,* the word that keeps coming back. I call
myself that, "little dummy"; something of sawdust belongs to sadness.

A man on his donkey sways by with fronds on the animal's rump.
They trot past the cave high in the cliff side. Black hole filled
with water's extravagances—bryozoa, crinoids, and corals.

Eons it takes to shift the sea bottom, until one day a next suddenness
appears on the horizon. Love is like that once, a brilliance
that calls to then darkens the eye for looking.

GARDEN SMILES

I sit in the courtyard of the museum café,
beyond the airtight displays of figurines posed
fetal, upright, and squatting—past the room dimly
lit for the mummies.

What should we make of the petrified body, of basins
bloodied by birth, then by slaughter? Not a good sign either,
those skeletons found with the skulls missing.

Aloof, the gods seem as unimpressed by killing as the waiter
is about wiping the table where I've finished lunch. I like to sit
under the pines, the doves cooing. Tall shade, clear tea, and about
us the widening rings of xylem and phloem.

On the grass, a baby drinks her bottle and looks this way.
Between sucks, she takes time for a grin, returning my archaic
curve of well-being.

TRAVEL

Moon floats over the Parthenon,

and I lean out my third-floor window to hear a man
yell and kick garbage around in the alley.

This could be why Sappho headed uphill to Kato Symi,

its cold, quiet streams at midnight.

Could she imagine from a distance lives waged in the city?

On the chapel roof there's a screech, then three shapes shift
into a cat and three kittens playing in the half-light. In turn,

they leap to claim, then slip from, the golden onion dome,

as through the vines comes a tom, in his mouth a fish swiped
from the corner market stall. He shakes it to get a better grip,
then jumps for a dark terrace.

For years Sappho toyed with the heart, mostly at night,
always near the water.

THE SWING GIRL

(O, to fly abroad again on her board roped to the limb.)

The territory that girl could cover, her eyes peering birdlike
across the grove. The air, a vector.

Return to the days of her swing, not this relic. To warriors
crossing the sea, ready to cross out generations with spears
then settle their weight down on this island.

Far past that sack of the sacred, I hear a donkey bray,
tied to the thorn tree. Empty snail shells bleach on boulders
near the tomb entrance.

(Old inching of the soul
               thirsty for a last sip of nightshade.)

Solemn, the child who set sail for the other side,
her funeral launch designed like a mouth curved upward.

(. . . slow to speak, hesitant to ask: why won't she smile anymore?)

The ossuary vessel is blunt, the remains are posed fetal
as if waiting to spring.
                       My crawl from the tholos tomb is as narrow
as the way in, then down the hot path past the unwatered donkey
and shells that held the damp curl of the living.

(After she died, the child was placed in her chamber—
               the swing and its girl tucked in beside her.)

ATTIC PORCHES

The dog paces, looking for a way off the ten-foot seawall
by the outdoor café.
                      Again he approaches the edge, whining,
ready to jump to me and my black coffee that won't stop
last night's dream from returning, the one where women

endlessly drop like spiders from a balcony to a far couple's bed.

From some high porch those women keep coming, carmine-mouthed
and petal-soft, not one of them fazed by the numbers involved in most
lovers' beds. And they're even less bothered by the quantity of worlds
I can hold in my head while eating toast.
                                    The profound sign for the void,
my book shows, is a mountain turned on its side, a circled cross at its top.
Almost like this +<, I suppose. The profound skew of last night
was the silence of so many mouths, open and falling.

MINOAN APOCRYPHA

Island   part of this
stepping-stone   path through the sea

shaded villas on the afternoon side of the mountain.

A washout.

Volcano, earthquake . . . no matter, the big wave kept
looming bigger, another plan for gardens upended.

The sea rose to crash foaming over the land. Young eunuch

leaping from bull back to bull back, his chosen path among many.

His studied balance quashed by water.
                                          So too, the gold
corn-brooches, tiara filigreed with the Bee. And those who
wore the jewels, and the crops and those who blessed
the crops—inundated.

The hearth proved no better than the swine trough
as into the courtyard Ondine's liquid smile descended.

This version of the sea stretched from island to island.

How to study loss closely? Always, the end is poorly
conceived, and this time it was thrust soakingly,
soppingly down upon them.

Cold blot on the day's shining.

Through the underbelly of a wave each creature rolled,
the far smear of daylight, granular and moony.

www.ingramcontent.com/pod-product-compliance
Lightning Source LLC
Chambersburg PA
CBHW022109160426
43198CB00008B/412